The Loooong Narrow Pharaoh & the Midwives Who Gave Birth to Freedom

by Rabbis Phyllis Ocean Berman
& Arthur Ocean Waskow
Illustrated by Avi Katz

"The old shall be renewed,
and the new shall be made holy."
— Rabbi Avraham Yitzhak Kook

Albion-Andalus, Inc.
P. O. Box 19852
Boulder, CO 80308
www.albionandalus.com

Design and composition by Avi Katz and Samantha Krezinski
Cover design by Daryl McCool
Cover illustration by Avi Katz

Manufactured in the United States of America

ISBN-13: 978-0692757215 (Albion-Andalus Books)
ISBN-10: 069275721X

The Looooong Narrow Pharaoh
& the Midwives Who Gave Birth to Freedom

by Rabbis Phyllis Ocean Berman
& Arthur Ocean Waskow
Illustrated by Avi Katz

Albion
Andalus
Boulder, CO
2016

Long looooong ago...

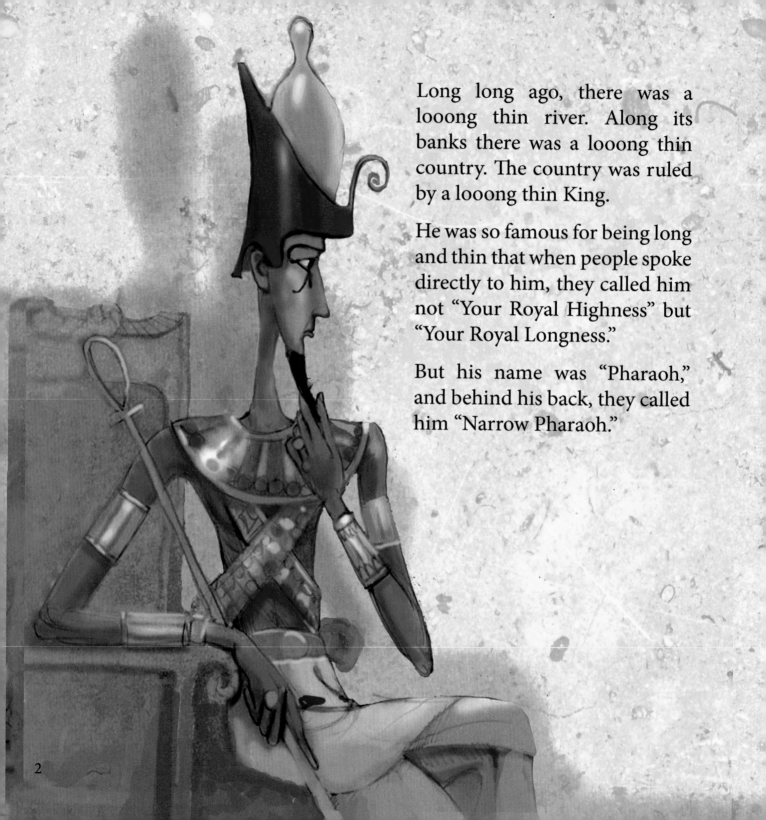

Long long ago, there was a looong thin river. Along its banks there was a looong thin country. The country was ruled by a looong thin King.

He was so famous for being long and thin that when people spoke directly to him, they called him not "Your Royal Highness" but "Your Royal Longness."

But his name was "Pharaoh," and behind his back, they called him "Narrow Pharaoh."

Pharaoh was long and narrow because he didn't like to eat.

"Eating is fun," he said. "And kissing is fun. And laughing is fun. Being a king is serious. It is not supposed to be fun!"

"Long and narrow is serious," he said. "But eating makes bulges. Bulges are not serious."

"No more bulges!" said the long narrow Pharaoh.

"I am long and narrow,

"My kingdom is long and narrow,

"And all my people shall become long and narrow!

"When I am not eating, no one shall eat.

"When I am not kissing, no one shall kiss.

"When I am not laughing, no one shall laugh."

One morning, Narrow Pharaoh looked out the window. There was a chubby little baby laughing in the grass. The King began to frown. "Babies make bulges, too," he said. "If you put a baby in a long thin woman, you make a bulge in her.

"If you put too many babies in a long thin country, you make a bulge in the country."

"I hate babies!" said the long thin King.

"They cry when I am not sad,

"And they smile when I am not happy.

"They eat when I am not hungry, And they smell all the time!"

4

So Narrow Pharaoh went to his high high throne. Up the steps he walked, five steps, eleven steps, seventeen steps.

When he looked very very tall, and very very thin, he spoke in a very narrow voice:

"Send me my Minister of Exact Justice!"

The Minister stalked in.

He was almost as long as the King, and his clothes were even longer.

He was almost as thin as the King, and nearly as narrow.

Said Narrow Pharaoh, "Tell me how to get rid of these extra babies!"

The Minister of Exact Justice raised an exactly shaped eyebrow. He raised it exactly three eighths of an inch.

"Let the babies grow up to be children," the Minister said.

"Then you'll be rid of them!"

"No!" said Pharaoh. "What good will it do if they're children? The children don't do what I say.

"They keep silent when I say 'Speak up!'

"And they whisper when I call for 'Silence!'

"They kiss when I say 'Hands off!'

"They loaf when I say 'Get your work done!'

"And they eat when I am not hungry!"

"Let the children grow up to be grown ups," said the Minister.

6

"No!" said the King.

"What good will it do if they're grown ups?

"The grown ups do what I say,

"But they laugh at the strangest times.

"They work when I say 'Work harder!'

"But they laugh when I say, 'I work hardest of all!'

"They fight when I say, 'Join the army!'

"But they laugh when I say, 'Death is glory!'

"They pay taxes when I say 'Make my palace richer!'

"But they laugh when I say, 'If my own bed is soft, everyone sleeps better.'

"It's good to have a big audience when I give speeches on the balcony," he said.

"But there are so many people they start talking with each other."

"It's good to have lots of soldiers when I need to march across the border," he said.

"But there are so many soldiers they might even join... with each other. And rebel against me!"

"There are just too many people for my long thin Kingdom.

"Tell me, Minister — get it right! What to do to win this fight."

And he glared hard at his Minister of Exact Justice.

The Minister's eyes turned gray, and his lips turned gray.

He spoke very fast: "Get rid of the extra people!"

"Oh," said the long thin King. "Now that would be exactly perfect! Why didn't you say so before?" And he threw a blanket over the Minister's head before he could speak any more.

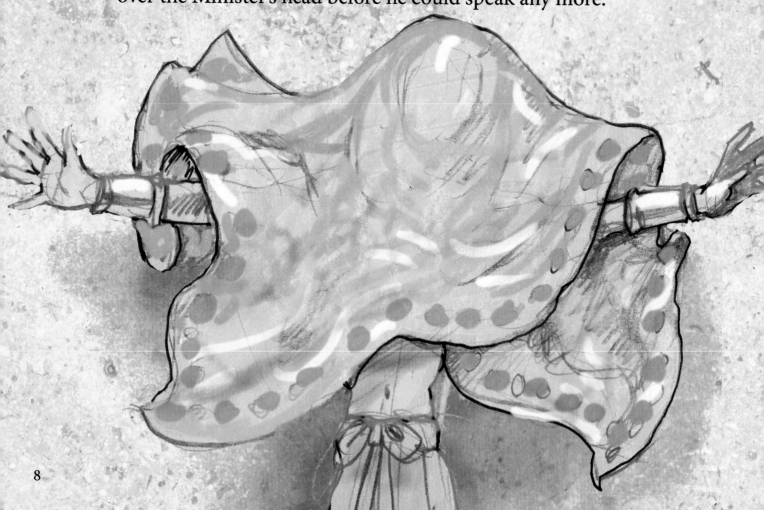

Then the long thin King called out in his narrow voice: "Send my Minister of Exact Numbers!

"Tell me, Minister Thin and Tight, "How to get these numbers right. "How many people are extra?"

So the Minister opened his Number File. Out came tumbling lists of numbers. Numbers of soldiers, and numbers of houses. Numbers of taxes, and numbers of milk bottles. Numbers of bedsheets and numbers of numbers. Innumerable numbers!

The Minister looked at all his numbers. He added them up and divided by 12, got a square root and subtracted 4 .

"Exactly six hundred thousand extra people," he finally said.

"In that case, Your Majesty," said the Minister of Exact Justice in a muffled voice from under the blanket, "I know exactly what to do. Up in the north are the Cross Over people. "Just four hundred years ago, a small band of them crossed over the Sea of Blood and started roaming around our country. They never settle down. They keep crossing over the Great Desert coming here, crossing back, crossing here, going back.

"When we treat them like foreigners, they get very cross. And when we treat them like home folks, they get very cross. So that's why we call them the Cross Overs.

"They have lots of babies. (Narrow Pharaoh turned slightly green.)

"They have lots of children. (Narrow Pharaoh turned slightly red.)

"And their grown ups laugh a lot at the strangest times. (Narrow Pharaoh turned slightly purple.)

"So they have grown and grown and grown. Last week there were exactly twelve hundred thousand of them. You could get rid of half and that would be exactly correct."

"If they're so cross, let's double cross them!" said the King — and he snickered.

So Narrow Pharaoh looked down from his very high throne. "Time to act," said Pharaoh sharply.

"Which half of the Cross Overs should I get rid of?"

And he glared at the Minister of Exact Numbers, who got out a page of records and began to read very nervously: "Half of them are grown ups, and half of them are children. Half of them are women, and half of them are men. Half of them have black hair, and half of them have red hair. Half..."

"STOP!" said Pharaoh. "I know! I'll get rid of the men. The men make trouble. The men are strong, and the men are always laughing. And the men ask questions when I tell them what to do.

"But the women are pretty, and they do what I say."

The Minister of Exact Justice frowned.

He opened his mouth to tell the King that the women might not just do what he said.

But the King was grinning. His grin was so wide the Minister thought the top of his head might come off.

So the Minister closed his mouth, and looked extremely worried.

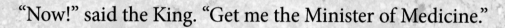

"Now!" said the King. "Get me the Minister of Medicine."

"Tell me, Minister, Long and Thin,
"How to get rid of the Cross Over men!"

"Start with the babies," the Minister said.

The King's face lit up; he felt even happier.

Said the Minister:

"Bring in the midwives
"Who help mothers give birth
"To their babies.
"Tell them to drown
"All the boys
"As soon as they're born.
"After a while
"There won't be
   any men!"

So Narrow Pharaoh clapped his hands. In came two women — named Shifra and Puah.

"Tell me, women long and thin..." the King began.

But then his voice faltered. He looked again at the women. They weren't especially long, and they weren't especially thin. Especially Shifra, who was short and schmaltzy.

Narrow Pharaoh looked itchy. Then he shrugged.

"Kill all the boy babies of the Cross Over people as soon as they're born!" said Pharaoh. "As for the girls and the women — let them alone. They're too weak to matter."

Shifra and Puah looked at each other. "Pooh!" whispered Puah. "Who said we're so weak?"

"Shhh," whispered Shifra. "Are you so sure we're strong?

"This is no time for talking. If we're strong, we can show it by acting."

So they bowed to Pharaoh. Then they stepped backward and backward until they were out of the Throne Room.

Shifra and Puah walked down a long thin hallway and out the palace door. "It makes me sad," said Puah. "But I suppose the King is the King. We're supposed to do what he says.

"Maybe he knows what he's doing. Maybe he has facts we don't have. There must be something bad about the Cross Over people. Or bad about boys."

Shifra shivered, and they kept walking through a great broad meadow, scattered with trees oranges and bananas, plums and quinces. They kept walking through the meadow till it ended at a riverbank. When they got close, Shifra looked at the river and laughed.

"I thought the river was long and thin —
"But now I see it is broad.
"It wanders and curls and bulges.
"I can hear it laughing at Pharaoh!
"I can hear it singing
" 'The Pharaoh is Narrow,
" 'And the river broad.'
"I think we should learn from this water."

Puah reached up to a plum tree. Its leaves rustled in the wind, and she leaned very close to hear its whispering. "The tree is breathing!" said Puah, and a plum fell, plop, at her feet. "I think we should learn from this breathing," said Puah.

So Shifra sat quietly listening to the river, and Puah sat quietly, listening to the wind. The two of them sat still for so long that a messenger ran up to say: "There's a Cross Over woman who needs your help to give birth!"

Shifra stood up. She took Puah's hand. Together they walked slowly down the riverbank till they came to the Cross Over village.

The mother was sitting in an open hut. Its roof was made of branches, and the walls were full of flowers. The mother shook and grunted and yelled. Shifra gently rubbed her back.

Puah said, "The wind will teach us. Breathe deep. Breathe deeeep. Breathe slow. Breathe sloooow. Breathe deeeep. Breathe sloooow. Breathe deeeep..."

Shifra said nothing, but when the birth waters broke she said, "The river will teach us," and held out her hands for the baby.

The baby was born — a boy. Tears of joy poured from the mother's eyes, and the baby began to suck at her breasts, to drink her milk.

Shifra looked at Puah. Puah looked at Shifra. Together they walked a little way off. They looked at the mother and the baby.

Shifra finally spoke:

"I am trying to see the King's face, but I can only see the mother's face . I see her face every which way. Tears of joy. Tears of sadness. The flow of the river in her eyes."

Puah finally spoke:

"I am trying to hear the King's voice, but I can only hear the baby's cry. I hear his voice over and over. Giggling, gurgling the flow of the wind in his breathing."

Shifra listened to the mother suckling.

Puah listened to the baby breathing.

"The King is strong," said Puah — "but this breathing is still stronger."

"The King is rich," said Shifra, "but this suckling is much richer."

"May this breath of life be King forever and ever," said Puah.

And suddenly around them everywhere they heard the Breath of Life. The palm trees were breathing. The crocodiles were breathing. The cat was breathing. The dandelions were breathing.

The moon was breathing. Everything was breathing.

The breathing sounded like this: *Yyyy-Hhhh-Wwww-Hhhh.*

"I will not stop this breath," said Puah.

"I will not stop this breath," said Shifra.

And they turned and tiptoed out of the hut and out of the village.

Eight days later, Pharaoh sent for Shifra and Puah. When they entered the Throne Room, his face was angry and purple.

"There are still boy babies in the Cross Over villages!" he said.

Shifra and Puah reached out to hold hands.

"I am a woman, and the mother was a woman," said Shifra. "I could not kill her baby."

"I breathe, and the baby breathes," said Puah. "I will not take away his breath."

"I can take away your breath!" said Pharaoh.

"You can take away our breath," said Puah. "But the whole world breathes. The King breathes, and the kingdom breathes. In and out, up and down. Now you are up. But you will come down. If you stop our breathing, then your breathing will stop. The Kingdom will stop."

"You can kill these births," said Shifra. "But the whole world is born. The King is born, and the Kingdom is born. If you stop birthing, you will have no more births. Your a-borning will die. The Kingdom will die."

"But I am the King. I can kill the whole kingdom. I can kill the Cross Over people, and everyone else besides."

"No, you can't," said Shifra and Puah. "We will not do it. No one will do it. We will help them to breathe, we will help them to live."

"There are too many of them already!" said the King. "My Kingdom is full of them. We are tight, we are narrow, we have no space!"

"Then let them come out from your Narrow Place, and let them break through the Red Waters, and let them be born! We are midwives. We know it is time for a birth."

21

"I will not! I will kill all of them, and I will start out with you!" said the King. "I will throw you in the sea to drown in its waters, I will cast you into the desert to die in its wind storms!"

"We are people of birth, not people of death," said Shifra.

"We will come to the sea and its waters will break, and we will pass through them a-borning. Death will pass over us!"

"We are people of breath, not people of death," said Puah.

"We will breathe in the desert and death will pass over us all!"

Pharaoh looked hard at them.

They looked hard at Pharaoh.

They turned to walk out of the room.

But Pharaoh began to laugh.

His laugh was ugly. It got louder and louder. It got screechier and screechier.

Suddenly it stopped...

"'Where is my Minister of Exact Numbers?" screeched Pharaoh. The Minister appeared.

"Tell them, Minister long and thin!
"Tell them what it means to win!
"Tell them how many Cross Over babies have died," screeched the King.

The Minister's face looked gray and tattered, like an old newspaper. He took a piece of paper from his pocket, muttered, "Five thousand seven hundred and forty six," and disappeared again.

The King glared at Shifra and Puah.

He snarled and he snickered, he snickered and snarled:

"Did you think you were the only way, when I had to do some kiling? A King has many hirelings when there comes a need for killing."

Shifra and Puah took a deep breath in. And out. In again. And out again: *Yyyy-Hhhh-Wwww-Hhhh.* Silently they stepped backward into the doorway of Pharaoh's Throne Room, backward and backward until they stood outside the palace door.

Shifra cried. Puah sighed. Shifra shook. Puah patted her. Together they walked down the hill and across the meadow to the great wide river at the bottom.

They sat at the edge of the water, watching it murmur and sob. Finally Shifra said, "So the babies are dying anyway. We must do more to save them. What can we do?"

"Talk to the women," said Shifra. "Women understand water. And wells and tears, and milk, and the waters of birth, and the waters of blood. The mothers. The girls. The midwives. The sisters. Not just the Cross Over women. Even Pharaoh has a daughter. She will not like this business of murdering babies. And there will be others. We two are not enough. But with all of us women together we can stop that King."

Puah was quiet for a long time. Then she whispered, "What about the men? Only women are people of water; but both women and men are people of air. Of Breath. Of wind. The King is killing the boys; it is really the men who are threatened. Why don't we talk with the men?"

Shifra shrugged. Shifra snorted. "Men?" she said. "The King is a man! It is harder for men to wait... firmly," she said. "They are not used to giving birth. They are not used to knowing when the time is ripe to act — and when the time is unripe. When it is unripe they are afraid it will never be ripe. So they stay quiet out of fear, not out of waiting. And when they cannot stand waiting any longer, they explode. They force the time, instead of growing ready for the birth. So they use knife to fight back, to make the birth happen."

But Puah persisted. "The King is a man, but only one man," she said. "The King has forgotten to breathe. But there are men who recall how to breathe. When my father held me close at his chest he would breathe — and his chest would rise and fall. He knew about rising and falling, he knew about holding me close, he knew about air and breath.

"We must gather the breath of all life. I will not abandon the men! They must learn to birth with their wives, they must learn how to grow and grow until it is time to birth without killing.

"And then they must teach the women that even the knife can be used for life. The knife must cut the cord, the knife must hallow the next generation."

So they went to the women and men. They talked to the midwives, the fathers and mothers. They talked to the sisters and brothers:

"We are no longer Cross Over people, for others will join us. We are a new people, we are just being born. We must have a new name. We must be the Pass Over people, so that death will pass over our houses."

They met with shepherds and teachers. They met with the King's youngest daughter. They met with a family of dreamers.

They talked, and they laughed, and they cried, and they argued. They sang, they whispered, they waited, they grew.

Some of the women said "Yes" and some of the women said "No." Some of the men said "No" and some of the men said "Yes."

Most of the Cross Over people said "Yes," but some of the Cross over people said "No." Most of the home folks said "No," but some of the home folks said "Yes." A few of the rich said "Yes," and some of the poor said "No."

So Shifra and Puah chose from the people they met with, and said:

"When the moon is round and full, it is time for us to give birth. That night we will meet at the river."

So the moon began to swell and the people began to stir.

On the night when the moon was full, the people made a circle at the river. The moon was round in the sky, and the people were round on the earth.

Shifra sat in the circle, and Puah sat across from her in the circle. The two of them said together:

"When a mother is ready to give birth, there must always be one man and one woman with her. The men must learn to give birth, the women must learn to cut the cord. You must go to the bank of the river, and you must sing to the water."

Then Puah nodded to Shifra, and Shifra sang this song:

"You are the water of drowning, and You are the water of birthing. Today you must give birth to life. Today you make peace with our children.

"And then you must make the sounds of the water: *Sh-sh-sh-L-l-l-l-Ommmm.*

Then Shifra nodde to Puah, and Puah chanted this chant:

"You must say to the air
" 'You are the breath
" 'Of the world.
" 'Our babies are born into you.
" 'You must be borne.
" 'Within them.'
"And then you must make
"The sound of the breath: *Yyyy-Hhhh-Wwww-Hhhh.*"

Puah paused. Then she looked around the circle. "Let us share our dreams," she said. "Dream new!"

One mother put her hand on her belly: "I dream that my child will draw us forth from slavery — and lead us to Pass Over the desert."

One father put his hand on his knife: "I dream that my child will teach us all — teach us how the knife can make holy, not dead."

A brother put his hand in the river: "I dream that my sister will dance through the water to freedom."

A sister put her hand on the thorns of a thorn bush:

"I dream that my brother will see light in these thorns, and give light to us all in our thorniest tangles."

Shifra called out to the princess, the King's youngest daughter.

And the princess said, "My language is different from yours, my words are different from yours.

"There is only one thing we share. It is breathing.

"Breathing comes first, before all words.

"Breathing comes last, when words are done.

"Breathing comes meanwhile; a breath is the word that includes all words.

"Our children will teach us to share our breath with each other, to share the Breath of Life."

And all the people said together:

"This Breath of Life will make death pass over us all.

"This Breath of Life will make us the Pass Over people.

"This Breath of Life will bring us out of slavery.

"This Breath of Life will become our King — and we will have no king."

And all of them rose to go back to their houses, to give birth to the Pass Over people.

When the moon was high in the sky, the people began to move.

From cities and farms, from palaces and shacks, came a great stream of people, a river of people.

From cities and farms, from palaces and shacks, came groans and shouts, a rushing breath like women panting to give birth.

The earth trembled, the houses shook, the people left.

They sang and they danced.

They blew breath into the horns of rams and goats, and the breath came forth as wails and shrieks of music.

They banged on drums and bells, and the blows came forth as rings and booms of music.

They plucked on strings and puffed on flutes, and all the sounds came forth as tunes of music.

"The world is upside down!" they sang, and then turned somersaults.

And when they came to the edge of a blood red sea the wind arose.

"Yyyy-hhhh-wwww-hhhh, Yyyy-hhhh-wwww-hhhh, Yyyy-hhhh-wwww-hhhh, Yyyy-hhhh-wwww-hhhh," the wind breathed in and out.

The wind pushed and the waters rose, the wind pushed and the waters rose, the wind pushed and the waters broke.

And the people danced across the sea.

On the other side, the people began to breathe together, making the sound of the wind. "We will never forget the sound of this wind this breath of life," they said;

"Yyyy-hhhh-wwww-hhhh, Yyyy-hhhh-wwww-hhhh, Yyyy-hhhh-wwww-hhhh, Yyyy-hhhh-wwww-hhhh,"'

33

RABBI ARTHUR WASKOW directs The Shalom Center (which he founded in 1983) and is the author or co-author of 22 books, including *The Freedom Seder, Seasons of Our Joy,* and *Godwrestling—Round 2.* RABBI PHYLLIS BERMAN is a Spiritual Director, recently retired from 36 years as founder and director of the Riverside Language Program, a renowned school for adult immigrants and refugees from all around the world. Together they have written *A Time for Every Purpose Under Heaven,* on celebration of life-cycle markers, and *Freedom Journeys: The Tale of Exodus and Wilderness across Millennia.*

AVI KATZ was born in Philadelphia and immigrated to Israel at age 20. Though perhaps best known as the illustrator and cartoonist of the *Jerusalem Report* since 1990, he is the author and illustrator of *Joseph and the Very First Cat* (2016), and has illustrated some 200 books in Israel and America. His books have won awards including the Hans Christian Andersen honors and the National Jewish Book Award. He is active in the international Cartooning for Peace organization.

43233934R00023

Made in the USA
San Bernardino, CA
15 December 2016